KURT CARR
ONE CHURCH
PROJECT

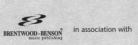BRENTWOOD-BENSON®
music publishing   in association with
GOSPO CENTRIC

CONTENTS

Reign

**Words and Music by
KURT CARR**

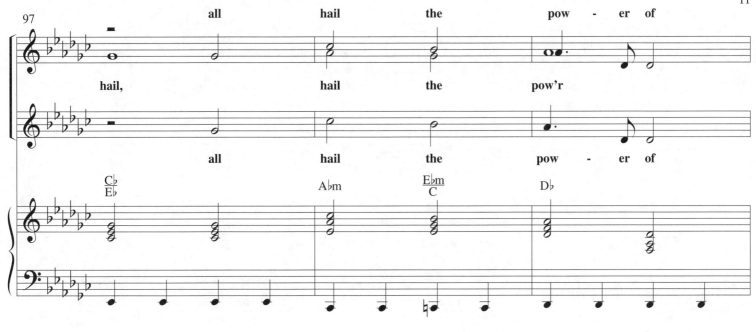

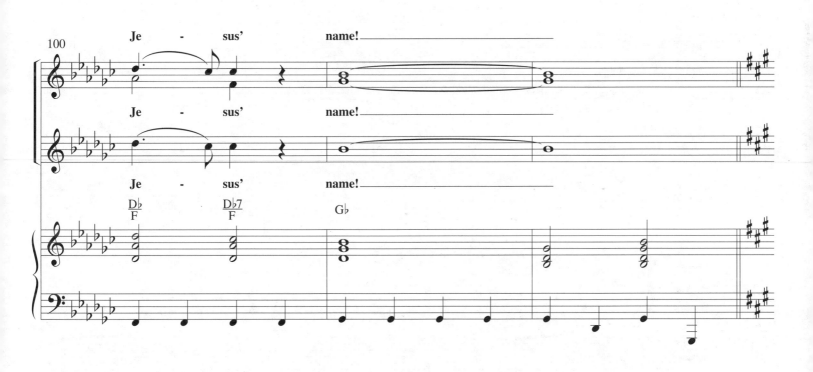

Hallelujah Praise
(Reprise of Reign)

**Words and Music by
KURT CARR**

God, Great God

**Words and Music by
KURT CARR**

With energy ♩ = 114

(opt. spoken intro over band)

(opt. Solo ad lib. fills throughout)

CHOIR unison

Glo - ry ___ and hon - or, ___ do - min - ion ___ and pow - er;

Now and ___ for - ev - er, ___ the Lord God ___ Om - nip - o - tent

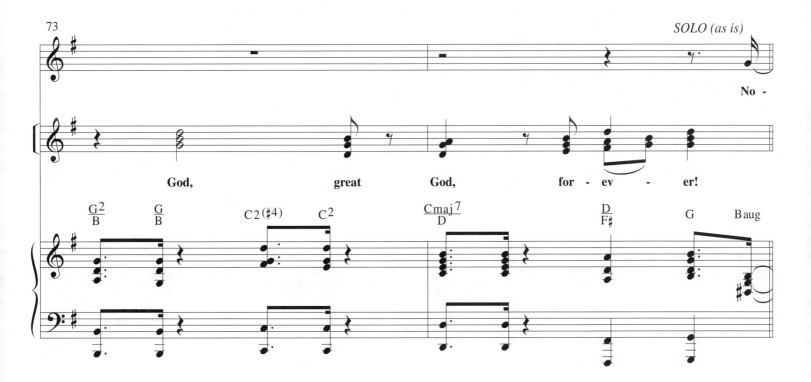

75

- bod - y great - er, ____ no - bod - y great - er, ____ no -

unison (at pitch)

No - bod - y great - er, no - bod - y great - er,

Cmaj7   C/D   Baug

77

- bod - y great - er, ____ great - er than my ____ God! _____ No -

no - bod - y great - er, great - er than my ____ God!

Cmaj7   C/D   1.   D/F#   G   Baug

1.

79

2.

- er than my ____ God! _____ Oh! _____

great - er than my ____ God! God, great

2.   D/F#   G   Ab2/C   Ab/C   Dbmaj9

Psalm 68 (Let Our God Arise)

**Words and Music by
KURT CARR**

Spoken: *The Scripture says in Psalm 68, "Let our God arise and His enemies be scattered.
As wax melts before the fire, so let the wicked perish in the presence of God." Listen!*

Fast Latin feel ♩ = 144

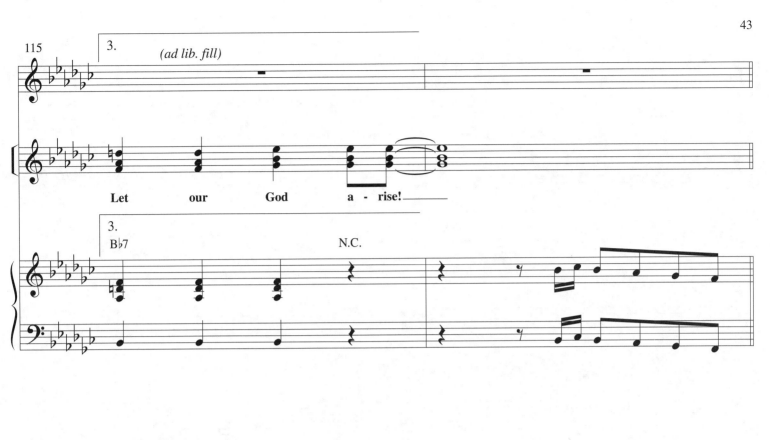

Let our God a - rise!

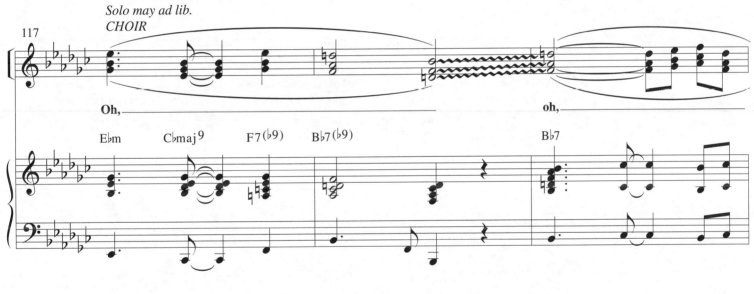

Solo may ad lib.
CHOIR

Oh, oh,

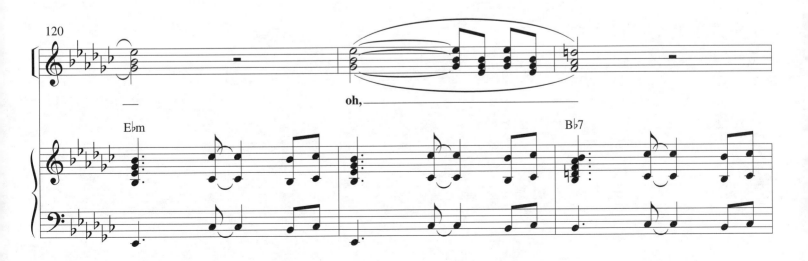

oh,

Power Praise

Arranged by Kurt Carr

God Blocked It

Words and Music by
KURT CARR

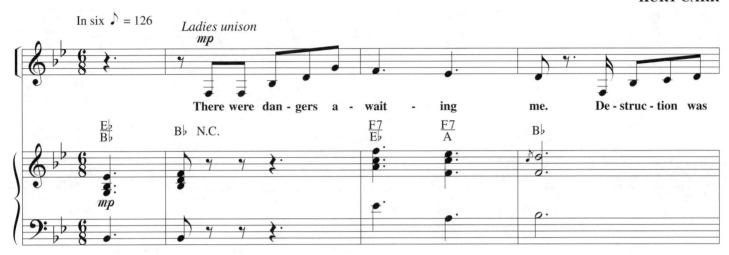

One Word

**Words and Music by
KURT CARR**

Spoken: *Dear Lord, as we prepare our hearts to receive a Word from You, please accept our praise, and receive this hymn as our offering unto You.*

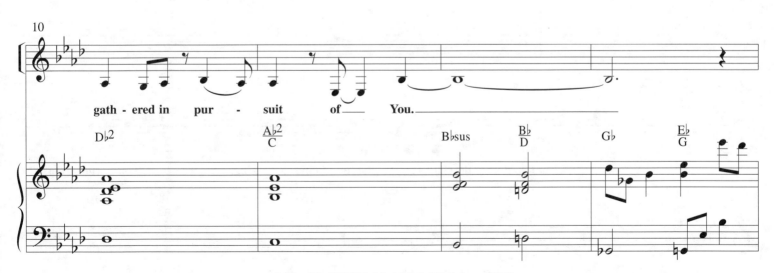

tai - lor - made___ for me.___

Ebm/C   F7   Bbm   Eb9

Ladies unison
mp

Speak, Lord,   speak, Lord,

Db/Ab   Gbm6/Ab   Db/Ab   Gbm6/Ab

mp

speak, Lord;   re - veal Your - self to___ me.

Db/Ab   Ebm/C   F7/A   Bbm   Gbm6/A

building

Speak, Lord,   speak, Lord,

Db/Ab   Gbm6/Ab   Db/Ab   Amaj9/B

building

Intro

**Words and Music by
KURT CARR**

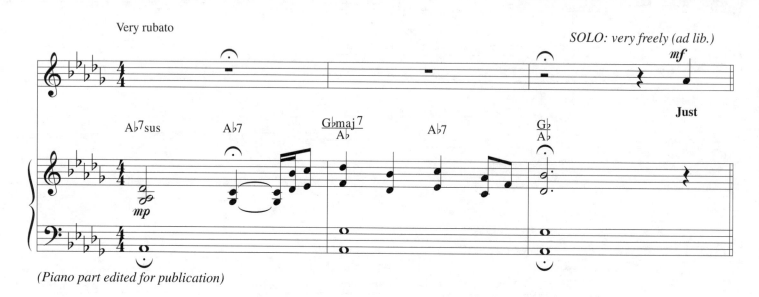

Speak, Lord Chant
(Reprise of One Word)

Words and Music by
KURT CARR

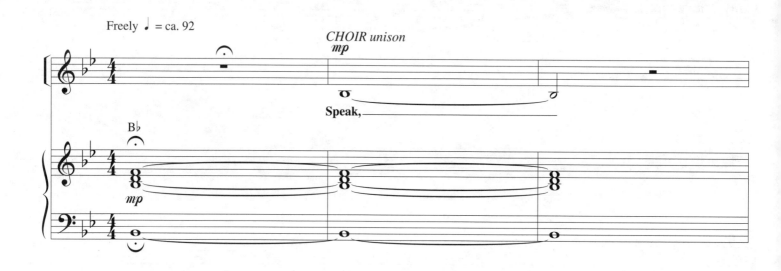

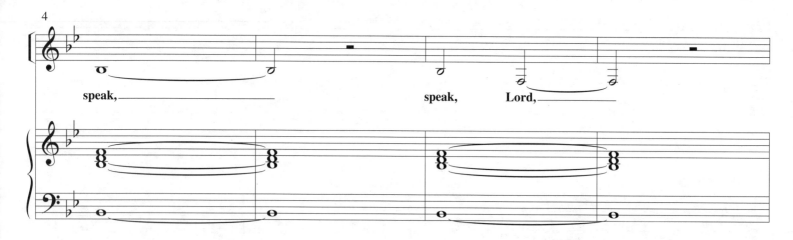

If I Tell God

Words and Music by
KURT CARR

Why Not Trust God Again?

Words and Music by
KURT CARR

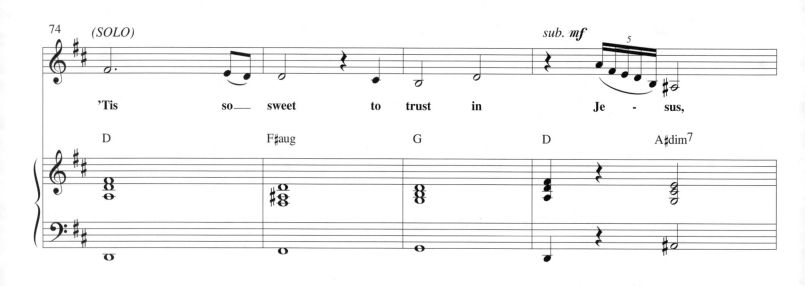

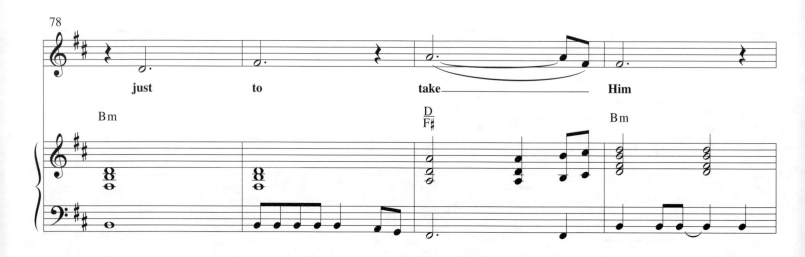

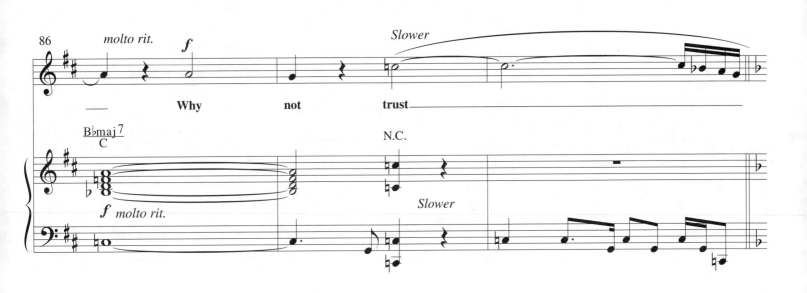

Be Grateful

Words and Music by
WALTER HAWKINS

My Time for God's Favor
(The Presence of the Lord)

Words and Music by
KURT CARR

Something Happens

**Words and Music by
KURT CARR**

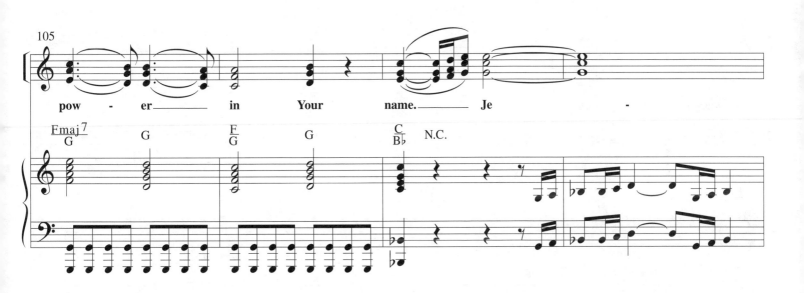

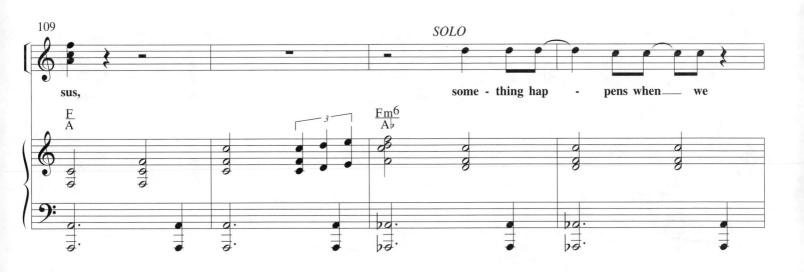

They Didn't Know

Words and Music by
KURT CARR

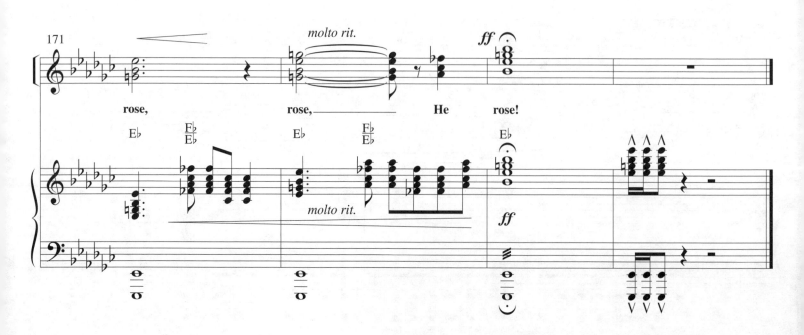